MAJOR LEAGUE SPORTS

LES SPORTS DES LIGUES MAJEURES



# MLB
# LA MLB

B. Keith Davidson

A Crabtree Branches Book

Un livre de la collection Les branches de Crabtree

Crabtree Publishing
crabtreebooks.com

## School-to-Home Support for Caregivers and Teachers

This high-interest book is designed to motivate striving students with engaging topics while building fluency, vocabulary, and an interest in reading. Here are a few questions and activities to help the reader build upon his or her comprehension skills.

### Before Reading:

- What do I think this book is about?
- What do I know about this topic?
- What do I want to learn about this topic?
- Why am I reading this book?

### During Reading:

- I wonder why...
- I'm curious to know...
- How is this like something I already know?
- What have I learned so far?

### After Reading:

- What was the author trying to teach me?
- What are some details?
- How did the photographs and captions help me understand more?
- Read the book again and look for the vocabulary words.
- What questions do I still have?

### Extension Activities:

- What was your favorite part of the book? Write a paragraph on it.
- Draw a picture of your favorite thing you learned from the book.

## Soutien de l'école à la maison pour les parents, les gardiens et les enseignants

Ce livre très intéressant est conçu pour motiver les élèves en difficulté d'apprentissage grâce à des sujets captivants, tout en améliorant leur fluidité, leur vocabulaire et leur intérêt pour la lecture. Voici quelques questions et activités pour aider le lecteur ou la lectrice à développer ses capacités de compréhension.

### Avant la lecture

- De quoi ce livre parle-t-il?
- Qu'est-ce que je sais sur ce sujet?
- Qu'est-ce que je veux apprendre sur ce sujet?
- Pourquoi je lis ce livre?

### Pendant la lecture

- Je me demande pourquoi...
- Je suis curieux de savoir...
- En quoi est-ce semblable à quelque chose que je sais déjà?
- Qu'est-ce que j'ai appris jusqu'à présent?

### Après la lecture

- Qu'est-ce que l'auteur veut m'apprendre?
- Nomme quelques détails.
- Comment les photographies et les légendes m'aident-elles à mieux comprendre?
- Lis le livre à nouveau et cherche les mots de vocabulaire.
- Ai-je d'autres questions?

### Activités complémentaires

- Quelle est ta section préférée de ce livre? Rédige un paragraphe à ce sujet.
- Fais un dessin représentant l'information que tu as préférée dans ce livre.

# TABLE OF CONTENTS



# TABLE DES MATIÈRES

# BASEBALL BEGINNINGS
# LES DÉBUTS DU BASEBALL

Baseball was developed from the British bat-and-ball games of rounders, stoolball, and tut-ball. The rules as we know them didn't start to take shape until the 1830s. The first baseball game was played on June 4, 1838, in Ontario, Canada.

Le baseball est une évolution de jeux britanniques qui se jouaient avec une batte et une balle : le rounders, le stoolball et le tut-ball. Les règles telles que nous les connaissons n'ont pas pris forme avant les années 1830. La première partie de baseball a été jouée le 4 juin 1838 en Ontario, au Canada.

## FUN FACT FAIT AMUSANT

The lowest attendance at a baseball game? The Florida Marlins set the record in 2011 with 347 fans showing up to see them play against the Cincinnati Reds. They blame Hurricane Irene, but the record stands.

La plus faible assistance à une partie de baseball? Les Marlins de la Floride ont établi le record en 2011 avec 347 partisans venus les voir affronter les Reds de Cincinnati. Ils blâment l'ouragan Irene, mais le record reste inchangé.

# AS AMERICAN AS APPLE PIE
# AUSSI AMÉRICAIN QUE LA TARTE AUX POMMES

After that Ontario game, Americans took over. Alexander Cartwright created the first rulebook—the Knickerbocker Rules—and baseball became America's game. Since then the game has spread around the world with leagues all through Asia, Europe, and Latin America.

Après cette partie en Ontario, les Américains ont pris le relais. Alexander Cartwright a créé le premier manuel de règles – le Knickerbocker – et le baseball est devenu le jeu des États-Unis. Depuis, le jeu s'est implanté partout dans le monde avec des ligues en Asie, en Europe et en Amérique latine.

William Rufus Wheaton was the first vice president of the Knickerbocker Base Ball Club.

William Rufus Wheaton est le premier vice-président du Knickerbocker Base Ball Club.

Knickerbocker Base Ball Club in 1847

Le Knickerbocker Base Ball Club en 1847

Knickerbocker Club

Le Knickerbocker Club

## FUN FACT FAIT AMUSANT

The Knickerbocker Base Ball Club was the first organized baseball club.

Le Knickerbocker Base Ball Club est le premier club de baseball organisé.

# ON THE MOUND
# SUR LE MONTICULE

Whether he throws a slider, a curve, or just a regular old fastball, the pitcher has to get the ball over the plate AND inside the batter's **strike zone**. If four balls are pitched outside the strike zone, the batter gets a **walk**.

Qu'il lance une glissante, une courbe ou simplement une rapide ordinaire, le lanceur doit lancer la balle au-dessus du marbre ET à l'intérieur de la **zone des prises** du frappeur. Si quatre balles sont lancées à l'extérieur de la zone des prises, le frappeur obtient un **but sur balle**.

A pitcher rubs mud on the baseball to get the proper grip, but not just any mud. Jim Bintliff found the mud and only he knows where to get it.

Le lanceur frotte de la boue sur la balle pour assurer une bonne prise, mais pas n'importe quelle boue. Jim Bintliff a trouvé la boue parfaite et lui seul connaît l'endroit où s'en procurer.

Pitcher's Mound
Monticule du lanceur

# BEHIND THE PLATE
# DERRIÈRE LE MARBRE

The catcher crouches behind home plate and has a great view of the infield. From here he can help the pitcher decide which style of pitch to use and also be on the lookout for runners trying to **steal** a base.

Le receveur s'accroupit derrière le marbre et a une excellente vue du champ intérieur. À cet endroit, il peut aider le lanceur à décider quel style de lancer utiliser et surveiller les coureurs qui essaient de **voler** un but.

The catcher receiving a pitch.

Le receveur reçoit un lancer.

The catcher is watching second base. He will throw the ball to stop the other team's player from stealing second base.

Le receveur se prépare à retirer un coureur avant qu'il vole le deuxième but.

## FUN FACT FAIT AMUSANT

The average baseball game uses 60–70 baseballs. In Major League Baseball, a ball's life is about six pitches.

Une partie de baseball nécessite en moyenne 60 à 70 balles de baseball. Dans la Major League Baseball, la durée de vie d'une balle est d'environ six lancers.

# ON BASE
# SUR LE COUSSIN

Each base is guarded by a baseman. Unlike the pitcher and the catcher, a baseman does not have to stay in his position. He runs to the high-action areas when **fielding** the ball.

Chaque but est protégé par un joueur de but. Contrairement au lanceur et au receveur, le joueur de but n'est pas tenu de rester à sa position. Il court vers les zones d'action pour attraper la balle lors d'un **jeu au champ**.

A baseman waits for the ball as a runner slides to base.
Un joueur de but attend la balle alors qu'un coureur glisse vers le but.

# THE SHORTSTOP
# L'ARRÊT-COURT

Standing between second and third bases, the shortstop position fields more balls than any other player on the diamond. A good shortstop is quick, agile, and has an accurate throwing arm to get the ball to first base when it's needed.

Se tenant entre le deuxième but et le troisième but, l'arrêt-court attrape plus de balles que tout autre joueur sur le champ intérieur. Un bon arrêt-court est rapide, agile et a un bras lanceur précis pour lancer la balle au premier but quand c'est nécessaire.

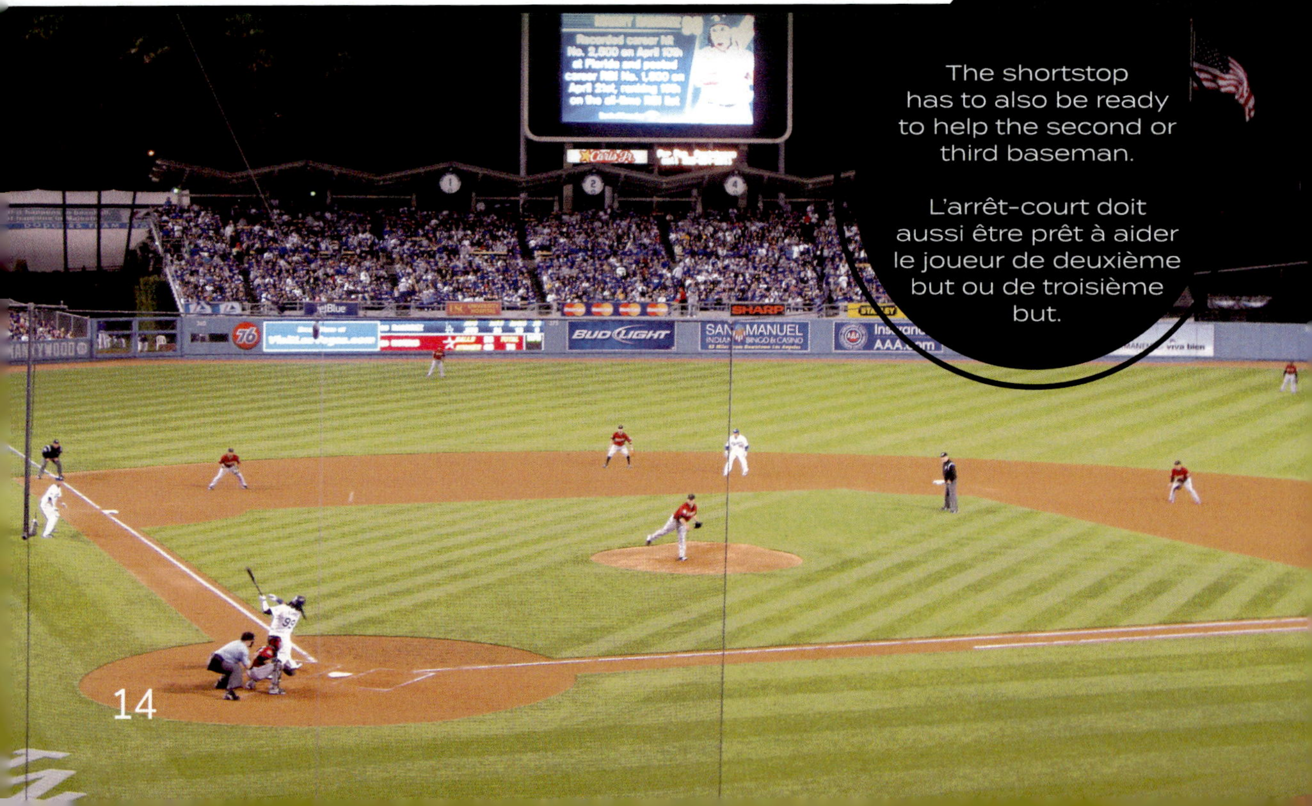


The shortstop has to also be ready to help the second or third baseman.

L'arrêt-court doit aussi être prêt à aider le joueur de deuxième but ou de troisième but.

During the 2000 season, Derek Jeter, playing for the New York Yankees, became the only player to win both the All-Star game **MVP** and the World Series MVP in the same year.

Pendant la saison 2000, Derek Jeter, qui jouait pour les Yankees de New York, est devenu le seul joueur à être nommé **JPU** au match des étoiles et à la Série mondiale au cours de la même année.

# OUTFIELD
# LE CHAMP EXTÉRIEUR

Chasing **fly balls** behind the bases, the three **outfielders** have a lot of turf to cover. One of the most exciting plays in baseball? When an outfielder runs to the back wall and jumps up to make a spectacular catch.

Poursuivant les **ballons** derrière les buts, les trois **voltigeurs** ont une grande surface à couvrir. L'un des jeux les plus palpitants au baseball? Quand un voltigeur court vers le mur arrière et saute pour faire un attrapé spectaculaire.

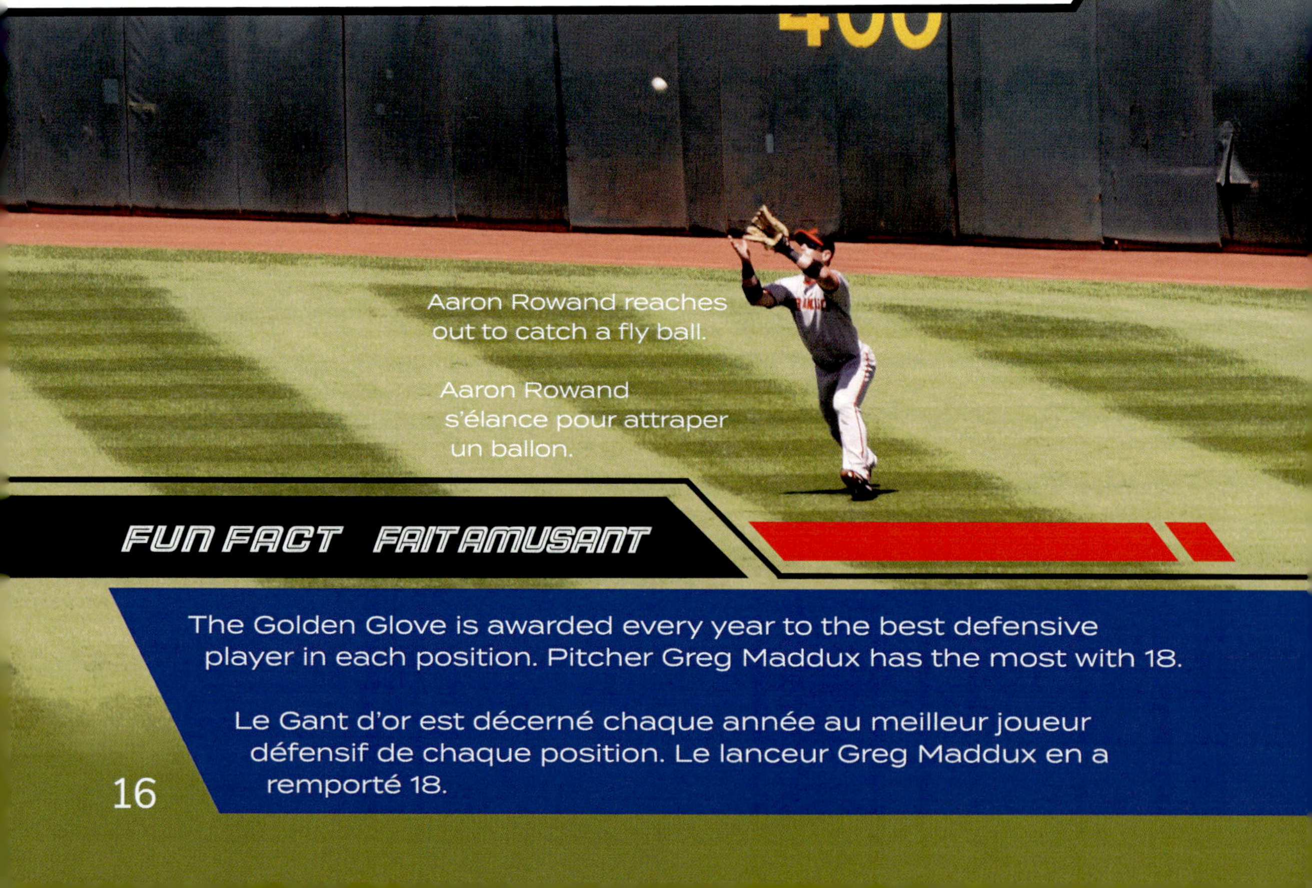


Aaron Rowand reaches out to catch a fly ball.

Aaron Rowand s'élance pour attraper un ballon.

## FUN FACT FAIT AMUSANT

The Golden Glove is awarded every year to the best defensive player in each position. Pitcher Greg Maddux has the most with 18.

Le Gant d'or est décerné chaque année au meilleur joueur défensif de chaque position. Le lanceur Greg Maddux en a remporté 18.

Barry Bonds

Barry Bonds holds the record for the most career home runs with 762.

Barry Bonds détient le record du plus grand nombre de coups de circuit en carrière : 762.

# SWINGING FOR THE FENCES

# FRAPPER UN COUP DE CIRCUIT

The batter tries to hit the ball over the outfield fence and score a home run, but there are many other types of hits. Grounders, line drives, bunts, and fly balls are all fair hits, as long as the ball doesn't go past the **foul lines**.

Le frappeur essaie de propulser la balle par-dessus la clôture du champ extérieur et de faire un coup de circuit, mais il y a plusieurs autres types de coups. Les balles rebondissantes, les flèches, les amortis et les ballons sont tous de bons coups, à condition que la balle ne dépasse pas les **lignes de champ**.

If a batter misses a fair pitch, he gets a strike. Three strikes and he's out.

Si un frappeur manque un bon lancé, il obtient une prise. Trois prises et il est retiré.

Javier Báez, shortstop for the Chicago Cubs

Javier Báez, arrêt-court des Cubs de Chicago.

Mickey Mantle holds the record for the most World Series home runs with 18.

Mickey Mantle détient le record du plus grand nombre de coups de circuit frappés pendant la Série mondiale : 18.

# UMPIRES
# LES ARBITRES

Four umpires are used in an **MLB** game. Behind the plate, an umpire calls the balls, strikes, and fouls. That umpire is also in charge of calling runners safe at the plate. The base umpires determine whether a runner is safe or out at the bases.

Quatre arbitres sont utilisés dans une partie de la **MLB**. Derrière le marbre, un arbitre signale les balles, les prises et les fausses balles. Cet arbitre est aussi responsable de déclarer les coureurs saufs au marbre.

When team managers argue with an umpire's call, things can get very heated and the managers often find themselves ejected from the games. Bobby Cox of the Atlanta Braves was ejected 161 times.

Quand les gérants d'équipe contestent la décision d'un arbitre, la situation peut s'enflammer rapidement. Les gérants finissent souvent par être expulsés des parties. Bobby Cox des Braves d'Atlanta a été expulsé 161 fois.

PUJOLS
5
19

25

# THE WORLD SERIES
# LA SÉRIE MONDIALE

An MLB season has 162 games. The season ends with the World Series, a series of seven games between the winners from the NL and the winners from the AL. The first team to win four games gets the Commissioner's Trophy.

Une saison de la MLB comprend 162 parties. La saison se termine avec la Série mondiale, une série de sept parties entre les gagnants de la NL et les gagnants de l'AL. La première équipe à remporter quatre parties reçoit le Commissioner's Trophy.

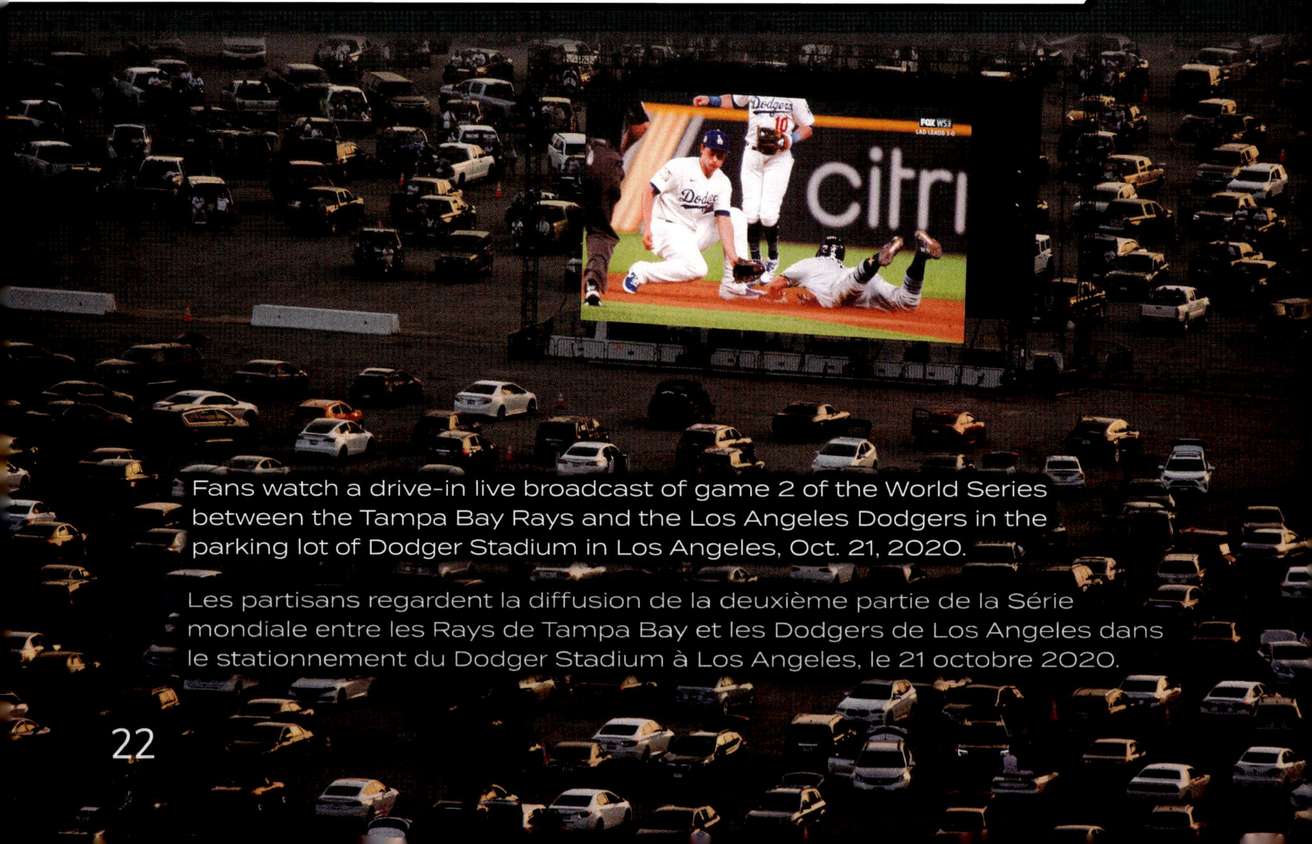

Fans watch a drive-in live broadcast of game 2 of the World Series between the Tampa Bay Rays and the Los Angeles Dodgers in the parking lot of Dodger Stadium in Los Angeles, Oct. 21, 2020.

Les partisans regardent la diffusion de la deuxième partie de la Série mondiale entre les Rays de Tampa Bay et les Dodgers de Los Angeles dans le stationnement du Dodger Stadium à Los Angeles, le 21 octobre 2020.

The Commissioner's Trophy is presented each year to the MLB team that wins the World Series.

Le Commissioner's Trophy est présenté chaque année à l'équipe de la MLB qui remporte la Série mondiale.

Yogi Berra has 10 World Series rings, the most by an individual player.

Yogi Berra a 10 bagues de la Série mondiale, le plus grand nombre de bagues remportées par un seul joueur.

# KEN GRIFFEY, JR.

CAREER 1989-2010
CARRIÈRE : 1989 À 2010

***POSITION***
**CENTER FIELDER**
***POSITION***
**VOLTIGEUR DE CENTRE**

| | |
|---|---|
| BATS<br>FRAPPEUR | LEFT<br>GAUCHER |
| THROWS<br>LANCER | LEFT<br>GAUCHER |
| HOME RUNS<br>COUPS DE CIRCUIT | 630<br>630 |
| BATTING AVERAGE<br>MOYENNE AU BÂTON | .284<br>0,284 |

# JOSÉ BAUTISTA

CAREER **2004-2018**
CARRIÈRE : **2004 À 2018**

***POSITION***
**RIGHT FIELDER AND THIRD BASEMAN**
***POSITION***
**VOLTIGEUR DROIT ET TROISIÈME BUT**

| | |
|---|---|
| *BATS* *FRAPPEUR* | **RIGHT** **DROITIER** |
| *THROWS* *LANCER* | **RIGHT** **DROITIER** |
| *HOME RUNS* *COUPS DE CIRCUIT* | **344** **344** |
| *BATTING AVERAGE* *MOYENNE AU BÂTON* | **.247** **0,247** |

# NOLAN RYAN

CAREER **1966-1993**
CARRIÈRE : **1966 À 1993**

***POSITION***
**PITCHER**

***POSITION***
**LANCEUR**

| | |
|---|---|
| *BATS* / *FRAPPEUR* | RIGHT / GAUCHER |
| *THROWS* / *LANCER* | RIGHT / GAUCHER |
| *STRIKEOUTS* / *RETRAITS AU BÂTON* | 5,714 / 5 714 |
| *WINS* / *VICTOIRES* | 324 / 324 |

# MIKE TROUT

CAREER **2011-PRESENT**
CARRIÈRE : **2011 À PRÉSENTEMENT**

***POSITION***
**CENTER FIELDER**

***POSITION***
**VOLTIGEUR DE CENTRE**

| | |
|---|---|
| ***BATS*** <br> ***FRAPPEUR*** | **RIGHT** <br> **GAUCHER** |
| ***THROWS*** <br> ***LANCER*** | **RIGHT** <br> **GAUCHER** |
| ***HOME RUNS*** <br> ***COUPS DE CIRCUIT*** | **302** <br> **302** |
| ***BATTING AVERAGE*** <br> ***MOYENNE AU BÂTON*** | **.304** <br> **304** |

# THE MLB
# LA MLB

Reaching the Major League is the dream of every young baseball player. It is the result of years of hard work and dedication. Start practicing now and maybe one day a kid will be reading an MLB book about you!

Atteindre la ligue majeure est le rêve de tout jeune joueur. C'est l'aboutissement d'années de travail ardu et de dévouement. Commence à te pratiquer maintenant et peut-être qu'un jour, un enfant lira un livre sur la MLB qui parle de toi!

**FUN FACT** **FAIT AMUSANT**

Deion Sanders played professional football AND baseball. He is the only person who has played in both the Super Bowl and the World Series. He's also the only person to hit a home run and score a touchdown in the same week.

Deion Sanders a joué au football professionnel ET au baseball professionnel. Il est la seule personne à avoir participé au Super Bowl et à la Série mondiale. Il est aussi la seule personne à avoir fait un coup de circuit et un touché dans la même semaine.

Barry Larkin of the
Cincinnati Reds

Barry Larkin des
Reds de Cincinnati

# GLOSSARY/GLOSSAIRE

**AL** (AY-EL): The American League of Professional Baseball Clubs that makes up half of the MLB
**diamond** (DYE-muhnd): The playing field used for baseball
**fielding** (FEEL-ding): Catching or stopping a ball that has been hit
**fly balls** (FLYE-ballz): Balls that have been hit high into the air
**foul lines** (FOWL LINEZ): The two lines running from home plate, through first base and third base, to the foul poles
**MLB** (EM-EL-BEE): Major League Baseball, an organization made up of two professional baseball leagues or groups: the American League (AL) and the National League (NL)
**MVP** (EM-VEE-PEE): Most Valuable Player
**NL** (EN-EL): The National League of Professional Baseball Clubs that makes up half of the MLB
**outfielders** (OUT-feel-derz): The three players that catch or stop the balls hit into the outfield
**steal** (STEEL): To move to a base without there being a batted ball or a walk
**strike zone** (STRIKE ZOHN): The area over home plate between the batter's knees and his shoulders
**walk** (WAWK): When a batter is awarded first base after the pitcher throws four pitches out of the strike zone, none of which are swung at by the hitter

**AL (é-èl)** : L'American League, la ligue américaine des clubs de baseball professionnels qui forment la moitié de la MLB
**ballons** (ba-lon) : Des balles frappées haut dans les airs
**but sur balle** (bu sur-bal) : Quand un frappeur reçoit le premier but après que le lanceur ait fait quatre lancers à l'extérieur de la zone des prises, sans qu'aucun n'ait été frappé par le frappeur
**champ intérieur** (chan in-té-rieur) : Le terrain de jeu utilisé pour le baseball
**jeu au champ** (jeu o chan) : Attraper ou arrêter une balle qui a été frappée
**JPU** (ji-pé-u) : Le joueur le plus utile
**lignes de champ** (li-gne de chan) : Les deux lignes qui relient le marbre au poteau de démarcation en passant par le premier but et le troisième but
**MLB** (èm-èl-bé) : La Major League Baseball, ou ligue majeure de baseball, une organisation composée de deux ligues ou groupes de baseball professionnels : l'American League (AL) et la National League (NL)
**NL** (èn-èl) : La National League, la ligue nationale de clubs de baseball professionnels qui forment la moitié de la MLB
**voler** (vo-lé) : Se déplacer vers un but sans qu'une balle ait été frappée ou sans but sur balle
**voltigeurs** (vol-ti-jeur) : Les trois joueurs qui attrapent ou arrêtent les balles frappées dans le champ extérieur
**zone des prises** (zonn dè pri-ze) : La section au-dessus du marbre, entre les genoux et les épaules du frappeur

# INDEX/INDEX



# COOL FACTS/FAITS INTÉRESSANTS

Cy Young holds the record for most wins by a pitcher with 511, and also the most losses by a pitcher with 316.

Jackie Mitchell, at 17 years old, became the only woman to strike out both Babe Ruth and Lou Gherig.

The rarest pitch in baseball is called the screwball. It's a breaking ball that heads in the opposite direction of the pitcher's normal breaking ball.

Cy Young détient le record du plus grand nombre de victoires par un lanceur avec 511, mais aussi du plus grand nombre de défaites par un lanceur avec 316.

Jackie Mitchell, à 17 ans, est devenue la seule femme à avoir retiré Babe Ruth et Lou Gherig.

Le lancer le plus rare au baseball est appelé la courbe renversée. Il s'agit d'un lancer de balle avec torsion du bras qui donne à la trajectoire une direction opposée à la courbe normale.

## WEBSITES FOR MORE COOL FACTS
## SITES WEB POUR D'AUTRES FAITS INTÉRESSANTS

Les sites Web sont en anglais.

www.sikids.com/baseball

www.mlb.com/fans/kids/activities

https://kidskonnect.com/sports/baseball

## ABOUT THE AUTHOR/À PROPOS DE L'AUTEUR


### B. Keith Davidson

B. Keith Davidson grew up playing with his three brothers and a host of neighborhood children, learning about life through sports and physical activity. He now teaches these games to his three children.

B. Keith Davidson a grandi en jouant avec ses trois frères et une foule d'enfants du quartier. Il a appris la vie par les sports et l'activité physique. Il enseigne maintenant ces jeux à ses trois enfants




# Crabtree Publishing

crabtreebooks.com 800-387-7650





**Written by/Auteur :** B. Keith Davidson
**Designed by/Conception :** Jennifer Dydyk
**Edited by/Révision :** Tracy Nelson Maurer
**Proofreader/Correctrice :** Melissa Boyce
**Translation/Traduction** : Annie Evearts
**Production manager/Coordinatrice à l'impression :** Candice Campbell

**Library and Archives Canada Cataloguing in Publication**
Available at the Library and Archives Canada

**Library of Congress Cataloging-in-Publication Data**
Available at the Library of Congress

Printed in the U.S.A./Imprimé aux États-Unis/CP112025

**Published in Canada**
**Publié au Canada**
**Crabtree Publishing**
616 Welland Avenue
St. Catharines, Ontario
L2M 5V6

**Published in the United States**
**Publié aux États-Unis**
**Crabtree Publishing**
347 Fifth Avenue
Suite 1402-145
New York, NY 10016

**Photographs/** COUVERTURE: COVER: Top photo Shutterstock.com/ Vasyl Shulga, players © KYDPL KYODO/Associated Press, PG 5: ©shutterstock.com/Matt Trommer, PG 6: ©Wheaton_PD, PG 7: ©NYKnickerbockers_PD, PG 8: ©itstock.com/33ft, PG 9: ©Debby Wong / Shutterstock.com (top), ©Mark Herreid / Shutterstock.com, PG 10: ©Arturo Holmes / Shutterstock.com, PG 11: ©Arturo Holmes / Shutterstock.com, PG 12: ©Eric Broder Van Dyke | Dreamstime.com, PG 13: ©Arturo Holmes / Shutterstock.com (inset), ©JASON TENCH / Shutterstock.com (top), PG 14: ©Eric Broder Van Dyke / Shutterstock.com, PG 15: ©Sports Images| Dreamstime.com, PG 16: ©Eric Broder Van Dyke / Shutterstock.com, PG 17: © Sports Images| Dreamstime.com (inset), ©Eric Broder Van Dyke / Shutterstock.com, PG 18: ©Eric Broder Van Dyke| Dreamstime.com, PG 19: ©Keeton Gale / Shutterstock.com (top), ©MantlePortrait_PD, PG 20: ©Demerzel21| Dreamstime.com, PG 21: ©Lawrence Weslowski Jr| Dreamstime.com (inset), © Alexa Sklar| Dreamstime.com, PG 22: ©Ringo Chiu / Shutterstock.com, PG 23: ©Gopheliad| Dreamstime.com, ©Googie man_https://creativecommons.org/licenses/by-sa/3.0/deed.en, PG 24: ©Jerry Coli| Dreamstime.com, PG 25: ©Paul Mckinnon| Dreamstime.com, PG 26: ©Jerry Coli| Dreamstime.com, PG 27: ©Mike Trout © Keith Allison https://creativecommons.org/licenses/by-sa/2.0/deed.en, PG 28: ©DFree / Shutterstock.com, © Sports Images| Dreamstime.com (inset), PG 29: ©Sports Images| Dreamstime.com

Hardcover 978-1-0398-6999-8
Paperback 978-1-0398-6987-5
Ebook (pdf) 978-1-0398-7011-6
Epub (ebook) 978-1-0398-7023-9